21st
Century
Skills Library

HEALTHY FOR LIFE
ROCK CLIMBING

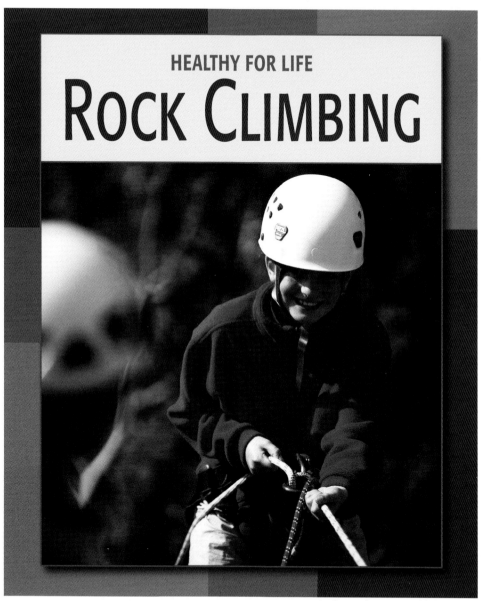

Michael Teitelbaum

Cherry Lake Publishing
Ann Arbor, Michigan

Published in the United States of America by Cherry Lake Publishing
Ann Arbor, MI
www.cherrylakepublishing.com

Content Adviser: Jeffrey S. Gehris, PhD, Department of Kinesiology, Temple University, Philadelphia, Pennsylvania

Photo Credits: Cover and page 1, © Anthony John West/Corbis

Library of Congress Cataloging-in-Publication Data
Teitelbaum, Michael.
 Rock climbing / by Michael Teitelbaum.
    p. cm. — (Healthy for life)
  ISBN-13: 978-1-60279-014-8 (lib. bdg.)   978-1-60279-088-9 (pbk.)
  ISBN-10: 1-60279-014-0 (lib. bdg.)   1-60279-088-4 (pbk.)
 1. Rock climbing—Juvenile literature. I. Title. II. Series.
  GV200.2.T45 2008
  796.52'23—dc22   2007003891

Cherry Lake Publishing would like to acknowledge the work of
The Partnership for 21st Century Skills.
Please visit www.21stcenturyskills.org *for more information.*

TABLE OF CONTENTS

CHAPTER ONE

GO CLIMB A ROCK!

Think you can brave a towering mountain cliff like this?

A **sheer** cliff rises in front of you, towering hundreds of feet into the sky. There are no stairs, no elevators, not even a marked trail showing the way up. Yet nothing stands between you and the top—except your will, your skill, the right equipment, and control over your fears. This explains why the sport of rock climbing provides thrills, recreation, fitness, and a great sense of accomplishment to its many fans.

Basically, rock climbing is exactly what it sounds like. You climb up a big rock, step by step, inch by inch, until you reach the top. The cliffs and mountains you're climbing may be lush with vegetation or white with snow. More recently, rock climbers have started to enjoy their sport indoors. Many school gyms, health clubs, sporting goods stores, and recreation buildings have climbing walls. These man-made walls have hand and foot grips to help climbers reach the top.

Many people enjoy rock climbing indoors on a climbing wall surface like this one.

Climbing is done by many experienced athletes in top physical condition. But young people and beginners can have fun climbing, too. Many indoor rock climbing walls have easier sections for beginners. Many physical education classes now include units on rock climbing. You can even have a rock climbing birthday party at some facilities.

A fearless professional rock climber makes his way up this icy slope.

Rock climbing is popular all around the world. People climb on famous mountains and also unknown cliffs.

Many outdoor climbers start by "bouldering." This involves climbing up a boulder that is at the base of a cliff. The boulder is small enough that the climber can jump off and land on the ground safely at any time. This is a great way to gain outdoor experience and confidence.

The most advanced climbers do what is called **alpine** free climbing. They climb on huge mountains in harsh, snowy locations. This requires great skill, **stamina**, and mental toughness.

But no matter where you climb or how much experience you have, if you want to go climb a rock, you'll need the right equipment and training.

21st Century Content

Did you ever wonder why candy makes some people seem to bounce off the walls? Sugar is a carbohydrate. And carbohydrates provide your body and brain with energy.

While exercising, your muscles use up stored carbohydrates. So eating carbs before rock climbing, or any sport, is important. If you don't get enough, you'll have a tired, heavy feeling.

After exercising, you also need carbohydrates to replace the ones you've lost. But some carbs are better than others. Carbs with nutrients and fiber, like fruit and whole grains, are much better for you than candy. Remember: you want to climb walls, not bounce off them!

Thinking carefully about your diet will make you a better athlete. Ask your parent, teacher, or coach for a copy of the food pyramid to help you get started.

CHAPTER TWO

WHAT YOU NEED:
EQUIPMENT AND TRAINING

In rock climbing, it's all about your feet and hands. So the right shoes are a very important piece of a climber's equipment. While hiking boots may be perfect for walking through the woods or even walking up a steep mountain trail, rock climbers need shoes designed just for their sport.

The right shoes are a very important part of a climber's equipment.

Climbers prefer shoes that are lightweight, soft, and allow them to secure their feet in small cracks in the mountain.

Climbing shoes need to be lightweight and soft, with smooth soles. They need to be extremely flexible so climbers can jam their feet into small cracks in the mountain's surface. The shoes should fit snugly so the climber can take a more secure step.

21st Century Content

Renting equipment is a good idea for beginners. Once you know you love the sport and will be doing it often, you can begin saving up for your own stuff. The rental prices below are for one day.

1) Climbing shoes: to rent $7, to buy $100–$150

2) Helmet: to rent $5, to buy $50–$90

3) Sit (or waist) harness: to rent $7, to buy $30–$80

4) Chest harness: to rent $7, to buy $30–$80

5) Rope: to rent $7, to buy $100–$180

6) Carabiners: to rent $1, to buy $5–$20

Rock climbers use their bare hands to grip the mountain or climbing wall.

10

The three main styles of climbing shoes are slippers (no laces), low shoes with laces, and high shoes with laces. The slippers and low shoes allow more flexibility, but the high shoes give better ankle support.

While special shoes are a must, rock climbers use nothing but their bare hands to grip the mountain. Digging fingers into cracks, crevices, holes, or ledges—anything to hold on to—is key to climbing. But hands get sweaty and slippery, so powdered chalk is also a must.

Climbers keep cloth bags of powered chalk attached to the back of their harness. Before reaching for a new handhold, a climber sticks his or her hand into the chalk bag, then rubs the excess chalk off on the side of the bag or by shaking or blowing on the hand. The chalk that remains absorbs the sweat so that the hand can find a secure grip without the danger of slipping.

21st Century Content

Stefan Glowacz of Germany is one of the world's greatest rock climbers. He started climbing at the age of fifteen and immediately fell in love with the challenge and thrill of the sport. In 1985, he won the first sport climbing competition ever held, called Sport Roccia, in Bardoneccia, Italy. At the Albertville Winter Olympics in 1992, he came in first in rock climbing, although it was an unofficial demonstration sport so no medals were given out. In 1993, after winning many tournaments, Glowacz decided he no longer wanted to climb competitively. He turned his attention to climbing simply for the fun of it. Since then, he has challenged himself at some of the tallest, iciest, and most difficult mountains in the world.

"I see rock climbing not just as a sport," Glowacz said, "but a way of life."

In 2004, at the age of twenty-two, Britton Keeshan became the youngest climber ever to complete the climbing of the Seven Summits—the tallest mountain on each of the world's seven continents. Reaching the top of Mount Everest, the tallest mountain in the world, was one of the highlights of this achievement. But Keeshan is not satisfied to dwell on what he has already done. He's thinking about the future. "Now that I did the thing I thought I couldn't do [climb Mount Everest], I have to find another thing," says Keeshan. "It's going to be a never-ending process to get to the next waypoint on this bigger journey."

Although the shoes and chalk certainly help with safety, the rest of the rock climbing equipment is used exclusively for safety and will be covered in the next chapter.

Training for rock climbing is made of up two parts: physical conditioning through exercises to increase strength, endurance, and flexibility; and experience gained by practicing the skills needed on real rocks or indoor climbing walls. Your climbing experience also helps build your confidence and mental toughness. The mental training for rock climbing is just as important as the physical part.

CHAPTER THREE
STAYING SAFE

When it comes to rock climbing, having the right equipment is extremely important.

In rock climbing, unlike some other sports, the right equipment is not simply about performing better or looking more like a pro. In rock climbing, the right equipment can save your life.

A rock climber's best friend is the rope. It's what holds you in place in case of a fall. Climbers wear harnesses that connect to the rope. Sit harnesses strap around the climber's waist and legs, creating a seat that supports the climber's weight. Chest harnesses strap over the shoulders and across the chest.

Sit harnesses strap around a climber's waist and legs.

Carabiners are clips that attach a rope to an anchor.

In case of a fall, the sit harness stops the climber with the least impact on the body. The chest harness keeps the climber in an upright position during a fall, which greatly cuts down on injuries.

The all-important rope is attached to the mountain using **anchors** and clips (called **carabiners**). There are many types of anchors, but

A rock climber checks her equipment before climbing up the mountain.

"passive" anchors do the least environmental damage to the mountain you are climbing. Some passive anchors include tapers and camming chocks. These chunky aluminum pieces fit snugly into cracks to support your weight without creating new holes in the mountain the way "active" anchors, like **pitons** do. Pitons are sharp pegs that are drilled or driven into the mountain. Both active and passive anchors provide loops that climbers can clip their harnesses and other safety equipment to.

The carabiner is a metal loop with a section that opens and closes, allowing it to clip onto the anchor's loop. Using carabiners, one end of the rope is clipped onto the anchor and the other end is attached to the climber's harness.

Most climbers work in pairs—the climber and the **belayer**. To "belay" in climbing is to anchor the rope that the climber is using. The climber's rope is held by the belayer, who uses a belaying device to secure the rope and help support the climber's weight in case of a fall.

If a climber should fall, the anchor, rope, harness, carabiners, and belayer safely stop the fall and support the climber's weight until he or she can regain hand and foot grips on the mountain. Communication between the climber and belayer is essential for safety. They must shout to each other to make sure all the equipment is ready before the climber advances up the mountain. However, as a climber, you are ultimately responsible for your own safety, so be sure to always check that your equipment is properly closed, locked, and ready for action.

As with most sports, you shouldn't even think about rock climbing without a helmet. A helmet not only protects you in case of a fall, but also

Rock climbers should always wear helmets, in case of a fall. It's a long way down!

protects your head from any crumbling rock or **debris** knocked down by climbers above you.

Rock climbing helmets should be lightweight. They should fit snugly but also have adjustable straps. A helmet should not block your vision at all, and it should have **ventilation** (small holes) so that your head doesn't get too hot. Sweat could fall into your eyes, and you may not always have a free hand to wipe it away!

One of the most important parts of rock climbing safety has nothing to do with equipment. Knowing your limits can save your life. Only climb rocks or walls that you believe you can safely navigate. Be patient. Don't rush yourself into trying something you're not ready for. With time and practice, you'll get better and move on to more challenging climbs.

Many rock climbers think of climbing as a lifestyle, not a sport. You have to set a goal and overcome obstacles. When you achieve that goal and reach the top, you feel great. But there will also be times when you make mistakes.

Every climber falls. The trick is to learn how to fall safely. As you fall, keep yourself in an upright position. Keep your legs bent and spread apart. Always try to be facing the rock so you can see if you are coming close to it. If you do swing toward the rock, use your feet to cushion the impact. And remember, your equipment and belaying partner will help stop your fall.

Above all, don't panic. Keep your head and follow these rules for safe falling. It's a good idea to practice a few planned falls and recoveries. That way, if you do fall accidentally, you will have already experienced the sensation. Climbing doesn't just test your body. It also challenges your mind. Falling is just another challenge which experience and mental toughness can overcome.

CHAPTER FOUR

BEING A GOOD GUEST: ENVIRONMENTAL RESPONSIBILITY

Part of the fun of doing your rock climbing outdoors is taking in the beautiful scenery. Being out in nature and catching breathtaking views from high up on a mountain add to the pleasure of the sport. But along

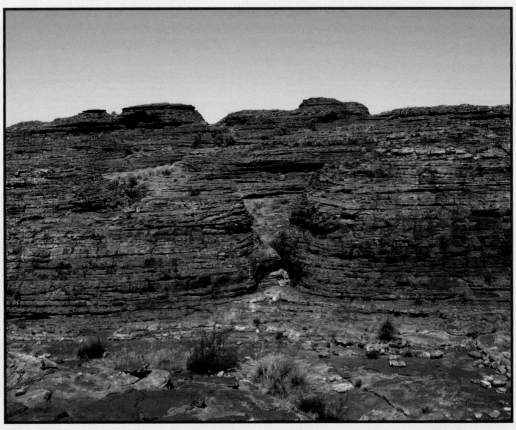

*Rock climbing is a great way to enjoy nature
and take in breathtaking scenery.*

*Designated climbing areas are safer for you and help
preserve the beauty of the surrounding area.*

with the use of beautiful natural areas comes the responsibility to protect those areas.

The easiest way to avoid damaging the rocks you climb on is to climb only in areas set aside for this sport. To you, a mountain may be the "field" where you play your sport. But to many plants and animals, it is home. You wouldn't like a bunch of strangers tromping through your house. So keep in mind that the rock you love to climb is home to part of what makes nature beautiful in the first place.

Climbers should be careful not to damage the area where they climb.

If too many people climb the same mountain, jamming their hands and feet into the same cracks, driving pegs into the same holes, great damage will be done. Animals lose their homes. Plants, which provide food for animals, will die off, leaving those animals with nothing to eat. Plus, dead plants lead to a loss of soil. Soon what was a thriving **ecosystem** is nothing more than a dead rock. By sticking to designated climbing areas, rock climbers can limit the damage to the area.

The same classic rule that is true for camping, hiking, picnicking, and visiting a park also applies to rock climbing: pack it in, pack it out. If you carry something in, carry it back out! In other words, don't leave any trash behind. Wrappers from snacks and empty water bottles should be carried out with you. Simply put: don't litter!

Garbage isn't the only kind of pollution. Noise pollution can ruin the good time of other climbers, hikers, and those also trying to enjoy the same natural beauty that you like. Don't play radios. Don't shout and scream and horse around with your friends. Be as respectful of the other people at the places you climb as you would like others to be in your home.

Here are some basic rules to follow when going to climb outdoors:

1) Only climb in areas designated for the sport.
2) Carpool. If you are going with friends, try to use only one car to cut down on noise, traffic, and parking congestion.
3) If you have to hike to reach the climbing rock, stay on designated trails. Never cut through the woods.
4) Keep all your stuff together and with you at all times. Don't leave packs or coolers strewn about.
5) Never carve into the rock or write on it with paint or chalk.
6) If you carry it in, carry it out. Don't litter.
7) Take only pictures. Leave only footprints.

These rules will help you be a clean climber. Clean climbing is a style of rock climbing that makes sure climbers don't hurt the environment. How else can you be a clean climber?

*With more options opening up, you no longer need to live
in or near the mountains to enjoy rock climbing.*

If you can't find an appropriate place to climb outdoors, don't worry. Indoor climbing places are springing up all over and can offer you a great climbing experience, with no fear of damaging the natural environment.

CHAPTER FIVE

THE ADDED BONUS: HEALTH BENEFITS OF ROCK CLIMBING

Sure you want to climb because it's fun. But climbing offers a bonus. It's good for you! Succeeding at this challenge builds confidence, not to mention muscles! But as with any sport, training your body to be ready is half the battle.

Rock climbing is a challenging sport, but it is also very rewarding.

Jumping rope is a fun and easy way to get in shape.

Regular exercise to improve your physical conditioning is key to training for rock climbing. It is very important to warm up before you train or climb. The easiest way to warm up is to run (even if you just jog in place) until you begin to feel warm or sweat just a little. Now your body is ready for the three most important parts of conditioning—strength, endurance, and flexibility.

Strength is gained by doing exercises to make muscles stronger. Muscles in your arms, legs, back, and stomach all need to be strong in order to be a good climber. It takes muscles to pull and push yourself up the side of a mountain. And doing strengthening exercises will help you get stronger muscles.

Endurance is built up by doing **aerobic** exercise such as running, swimming, or jumping rope for at least a half hour. The last thing you can afford while climbing is to get out of breath. Aerobic exercise is also great for your heart, the most important muscle in your body.

How can you share climbing with your friends? Mobile climbing walls have become popular for big parties, picnics, and planned group events. These walls are usually between 24 and 32 feet (7.3 and 9.8 m) tall and can be pulled by a truck to any location. Then the wall is shifted into its vertical position, ready for climbers!

Another way to climb with your friends is to become belay partners. Belaying requires trust and communication. The belayer has responsibility for the safety of the climber. Take turns climbing and belaying. Helping each other climb forms a great bond.

Drinking plenty of water is important for rock climbers.

Flexibility is improved through stretching exercises. Your arms, legs, shoulders, back, and fingers all need to be flexible. This is essential for being able to bend your body to fit the shape of the rock you are climbing, to flex your fingers so you get a good grip in a narrow crack, and to reach holds that might be a distance away. If you stretch, your muscles get healthier and you are less likely to get injured.

The second part of training comes from practicing climbing itself. As you progress from a beginner on low boulders or simple indoor walls to steeper mountains and more advanced indoor walls, your skills will improve.

Nutrition is also key. The food you eat is the fuel your body uses to do the job of getting you up the rock. Whole grain carbohydrates are important. So is limiting the amount of fat you eat. And be sure to drink plenty of water before, during, and after exercising or climbing. Keeping your body **hydrated** is essential to good nutrition and healthy enjoyment of the sport.

So what are you waiting for? Go climb a rock!

21st Century Content

Compare the number of calories a 100-pound (45-kg) person burns in one hour of rock climbing to the number burned in one hour of these other activities. If you weigh less, you'll burn fewer calories in the same amount of time. If you weigh more, you'll burn more calories in the same amount of time.

Rock climbing: 498

Playing basketball: 498

Running: 456

Backpacking: 318

Swimming: 276

Bowling: 138

Playing Frisbee: 138

Brushing your teeth: 114

Talking on the phone: 48

Watching TV or playing video games: 48

Glossary

aerobic (uh-ROW-bik) increases the heart rate for an extended period of time

alpine (AL-pine) of or relating to mountains

anchors (ANG-kurz) devices that fit securely into a crack on a mountain to help support a climber

belayer (bih-LAY-uhr) the person who holds the rope to help secure another climber

carabiners (ka-ra-BEAN-uhrz) rock climbing clips

debris (duh-BREE) fragments, wreckage, or garbage

ecosystem (EE-ko-sis-tum) a community of plants and animals and the environment in which they live

harnesses (HAR-nuh-sez) sets of straps for securing someone for safety

hydrated (HYE-dray-tud) having enough water

pitons (PEE-tahnz) rock climbing pegs

sheer (SHEER) steep

stamina (STAM-ih-nuh) staying power

ventilation (ven-tuh-LAY-shun) exposure to air

FOR MORE INFORMATION

Books

Dean, Cynthia A. *Rock Climbing: Making It to the Top.*
Mankato, MN: Red Brick Learning, 2006.

Graf, Mike. *Rock Climbing. Cover-to-Cover Books.* Des
Moines, IA: Perfection Learning, 2004.

Long, John. *How to Rock Climb!.* Guilford, CT: Falcon, 1998.

Oxlade, Chris. *Rock Climbing. Extreme Sports.* Minneapolis: Lerner Publishing, 2003.

Seeberg, Tim. *Rock Climbing. Kid's Guides to the Outdoors.*
Mankato, MN: The Child's World, 2004.

Web Sites

Rock Climbing Equipment and Techniques
alumnus.caltech.edu/~sedwards/climbing/
Descriptions and illustrations of rock climbing equipment and techniques

ABC-of-Rock Climbing
www.abc-of-rockclimbing.com/
The basics of rock climbing

Indoor Rock Climbing
www.indoorclimbing.com/
Listing of locations and resources for indoor climbing

INDEX

ABOUT THE AUTHOR

Michael Teitelbaum has been a writer and editor of children's books and magazines for more than twenty years. He was editor of *Little League Magazine for Kids;* is the author of a two-volume encyclopedia on the Baseball Hall of Fame, published by Grolier; and was the writer/project editor of *Breaking Barriers: In Sports, In Life,* a character education program based on the life of Jackie Robinson, created for Scholastic Inc. and Major League Baseball. Michael is the author of *Great Moments in Women's Sports,* published by Gareth Stevens, and *Sports in America: The 1980s,* published by Facts on File. His latest work of fiction is *The Scary States of America,* published by Delacorte in 2007. Michael and his wife, Sheleigah, live in New York City, where they root for the Mets.